I Love My Pet
HEDGEHOG

Aaron Carr

www.av2books.com

LET'S READ

AV²
BY WEIGL™

ADDED VALUE • AUDIO VISUAL

Go to **www.av2books.com**, and enter this book's unique code.

BOOK CODE

R 5 2 3 4 1 7

AV² by Weigl brings you media enhanced books that support active learning.

AV² provides enriched content that supplements and complements this book. Weigl's AV² books strive to create inspired learning and engage young minds in a total learning experience.

Your AV² Media Enhanced books come alive with...

Audio
Listen to sections of the book read aloud.

Video
Watch informative video clips.

Embedded Weblinks
Gain additional information for research.

Try This!
Complete activities and hands-on experiments.

Key Words
Study vocabulary, and complete a matching word activity.

Quizzes
Test your knowledge.

Slide Show
View images and captions, and prepare a presentation.

... and much, much more!

Published by AV² by Weigl —
350 5ᵗʰ Avenue, 59ᵗʰ Floor New York, NY 10118
Website: www.av2books.com www.weigl.com

Library of Congress Cataloguing in Publication data available upon request.
Fax 1-866-449-3445 for the attention of the Publishing Records department.

ISBN 978-1-62127-297-7 (hardcover)
ISBN 978-1-62127-301-1 (softcover)

Printed in the United States of America in North Mankato, Minnesota
1 2 3 4 5 6 7 8 9 0 16 15 14 13 12

122012
WEP301112

Senior Editor: Aaron Carr   Art Director: Terry Paulhus

Weigl acknowledges Getty Images as the primary image supplier for this title.

I Love My Pet
HEDGEHOG

CONTENTS

I love my pet hedgehog.
I take good care of her.

5

6

My pet hedgehog could not see
or hear when she was born.
She weighed less than 1 ounce.

8

My pet hedgehog was 8 weeks old when she came to live with me. She was full grown after just six months.

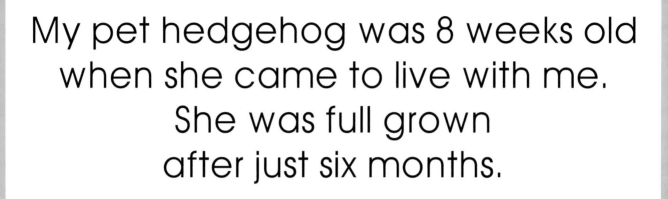

Hedgehogs can grow up to 12 inches long.

My pet hedgehog
is covered with spikes.
She rolls into a ball
when she gets scared.

My pet hedgehog
sleeps during the day.
She wakes up
and moves around at night.

In nature,
hedgehogs sleep
through winter.

13

My pet hedgehog needs to eat once a day. I feed her special hedgehog food.

Hedgehogs like to eat insects.

My pet hedgehog stays in a large cage. She has lots of room to run and play.

My pet hedgehog likes to be clean. She uses her tongue to clean herself.

Hedgehogs may sometimes need to be bathed.

I make sure
my pet hedgehog is healthy.
I love my pet hedgehog.

HEDGEHOG FACTS

These pages provide more detail about the interesting facts found in the book. They are intended to be used by adults as a learning support to help young readers round out their knowledge of each animal featured in the *I Love My Pet* series.

Pages 4–5

I love my pet hedgehog. I take good care of her. There are about 15 different kinds of hedgehogs. The African pygmy hedgehog is the species most often kept as a pet in North America. This hedgehog is also known as the four-toed hedgehog. Hedgehogs make good pets, but they require regular care and attention. Pet hedgehogs can live up to 10 years.

Pages 6–7

My pet hedgehog could not see or hear when she was born. She weighed less than 1 ounce (28 grams). Hedgehogs are born with their eyes and ears closed. Baby hedgehogs, called hoglets, weigh just 0.4 to 0.7 ounces (12 to 18 grams). Hoglets depend on their mother. She cleans, protects, and feeds her hoglets.

Pages 8–9

My pet hedgehog came to live with me at 8 weeks old. She was full grown after just six months. Hoglets continue to drink their mother's milk for up to eight weeks. Then, they are ready to live on their own. This is the best time to take a pet hedgehog to its new home. Full-grown hedgehogs can grow up to 12 inches (30 centimeters) long and weigh more than 2 pounds (1 kilogram).

Pages 10–11

My pet hedgehog is covered with spikes. She rolls into a ball when she gets scared. Within the first few days after birth, the hedgehog grows spikes, called quills. The quills cover most of its body. Between eight weeks and six months of age, a hedgehog loses its baby quills and grows its adult quills. When a hedgehog feels scared, it curls into a ball with its quills facing out for protection.

My pet hedgehog sleeps during the day. She wakes up and moves around at night. Hedgehogs are most active at night. Hedgehogs like to hide when they sleep, so be sure to give your pet plenty wood shavings for bedding. In nature, hedgehogs hibernate through winter. During hibernation, a hedgehog's heartbeat drops from 190 beats per minute to 20 beats per minute.

My pet hedgehog needs to eat once a day. I feed her special hedgehog food. Hedgehogs are insectivores, or insect eaters. Hedgehogs can also eat special food pellets that can be bought at pet stores. These pellets help keep the hedgehog's teeth clean. Never feed a pet hedgehog insects from your yard. They may contain germs or chemicals that can harm your hedgehog.

My pet hedgehog stays in a large cage. She has lots of room to run and play. A hedgehog cage should give them at least 1 square yard (1 square meter) of space. The cage should have a lid to keep the hedgehog from climbing out. The cage should be set in a quiet place during the day, away from direct sunlight.

My pet hedgehog likes to be clean. She uses her tongue to clean herself. Hedgehogs are very clean animals, but they may sometimes need a bath. Use a small bowl or a sink with 1 inch (2.5 cm) of water for the bath. Hedgehogs should also have their cages cleaned every day to remove soiled bedding or droppings, with a more thorough cleaning once a week.

I make sure my pet hedgehog is healthy. I love my pet hedgehog. With proper cleaning for both the hedgehog and her cage, and plenty of play time, hedgehogs should stay healthy and happy for many years. If your hedgehog begins acting differently, such as eating less or moving more slowly, take it to a veterinarian for a checkup.

KEY WORDS

Research has shown that as much as 65 percent of all written material published in English is made up of 300 words. These 300 words cannot be taught using pictures or learned by sounding them out. They must be recognized by sight. This book contains 54 common sight words to help young readers improve their reading fluency and comprehension. This book also teaches young readers several important content words, such as proper nouns. These words are paired with pictures to aid in learning and improve understanding.

Page	Sight Words First Appearance
4	good, her, I, my, of, take
7	could, hear, not, or, see, she, than, was, when
9	after, came, can, grown, just, live, long, me, old, to, up, with
11	a, gets, into, is
12	and, around, at, day, in, moves, night, the, through
15	eat, food, like, needs, once
17	has, large, play, run
18	be, may, sometimes, uses
21	make

Page	Content Words First Appearance
4	hedgehog, pet
7	ounce
9	inches, months, six, weeks
11	ball, spikes
12	during, nature, winter
15	insects, special
17	cage, lots, room
18	clean, tongue
21	healthy

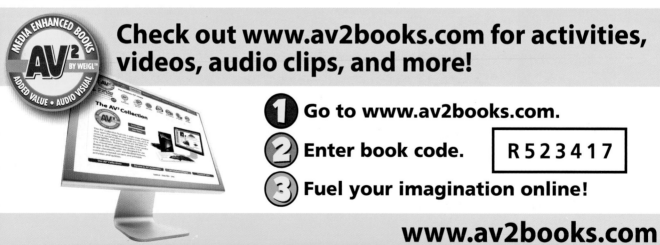

Check out www.av2books.com for activities, videos, audio clips, and more!

1 Go to www.av2books.com.

2 Enter book code. R 5 2 3 4 1 7

3 Fuel your imagination online!

www.av2books.com

5018